She Believes...

Uniquely Designed with Purpose in Mind

by Missy Helderman

GATEWAY PRESS

A Division of Aion Group Multimedia
and Gateway International Bible Institute

SHE BELIEVES
ISBN# 978-0-9915657-4-0
Cover Photo: Becky Boyles
Illustrations by: Amy Jordan

Published by:

GATEWAY PRESS
A Division of Aion Group Multimedia
and Gateway International Bible Institute

20118 N 67th Ave
Suite 300-446
Glendale, Arizona 85308
www.aionmultimedia.com

FOREWORD

Missy has created an avenue to lead us *not* only into the discovery of who we are but into an understanding of how the Father sees us. In the pages of this beautiful book, you will be lead into a deep discovery of your inner workings and you will finally understand your beauty and your worth to this world and to the Father himself. Missy has tapped into truths that are often misunderstood about ourselves and about those around us. I am particularly thankful for the chapter on our thoughts and how she relates them to living in a high-end condominium protected by a doorman. She teaches us to keep our thoughts secure from intruders that lie about our identity and wreak havoc on our beliefs about our worth and value.

I highly recommend taking your time to not only read this book, but to do the work of reflection that is required to take you from tricycle and training wheels to tandem stoker without living in fear of where the road may take you. As you do this you will be lead directly into the Savior's arms of love and you will ride smoothly down the road of freedom.

Blessings,

Dr. Dawn Brown,

Pastor, Skyway Church;- Apostle,- ASCEND Int. Ministries.

ENDORSEMENTS

"God takes each of us through a journey of discovery, a journey of connecting with our heavenly Father and growing into who He has created us to be. I firmly believe God has created each of us as a beautiful daughter with a unique and fulfilling destiny. Missy does an excellent job of guiding the reader of "She Believes" into a graceful and anointed process of personal growth and spiritual encounter with destiny. I highly recommend this book to all women who desire to live a life beyond the limits and kingdom adventure."

Rebecca Greenwood

President, Christian Harvest International - Strategic Prayer Action Network

"She Believes' is a practical guide to understanding and embracing your God-given destiny. Missy Helderman has a unique gifting to connect the dots, bringing fresh revelation for women who feel stuck and need someone to help them discover God's plans and purposes for their life."

Lynn Alderson,

President & Co-Founder, Kingdom Authority Ministries, Inc.

"Missy Helderman's, 'She Believes' is an inspiring small book with big concepts about the journey we all face. A journey that brings us to the heart of who we are and what we were destined to be. A delightful quick read that will encourage and inspire! I found it enlightening and thought provoking." ~

Dr. Dallas Eggemeyer,

Lightbearers International, Atlanta, GA

"God has designed you with everything you need to fulfill your kingdom purpose. You were created with a unique personality, passion, set of talents, skills, and dreams. He has placed them inside of you from the beginning to achieve what you were created to be. Missy Helderman's book 'She Believes' is creatively written to help everyone understand how they are wired by God with a wonderful collection of gifts, talents, personality traits, and experiences that will equip them to become the very best God made them to be."

Dr Brian Alton

Founder of Gateway International Bible Institute;
Bishop / Senior Pastor Desert Rose Community Church, Peoria, AZ.

"If you truly desire to discover, understand, and embrace your God-given design, then this book is the key to unlock that process for you. 'She Believes' takes you on a transformative journey that will challenge and inspire you to draw closer to God in order to reflect His glory and to live out your purpose. With practical and powerful insight that can only be gained by going through the fire and emerging refined + renewed, Missy shares tools, strategies and prayers that work! Her heart for seeing women experience true freedom, healing, and wholeness is evident on every page. I have no doubt that God is going to use this book to encourage, uplift and launch His daughters into greatness."

Ilesha "CoCo" Graham

Speaker + Founder, Flourishing Women Ministries

ACKNOWLEDGMENTS

To these I offer my heartfelt thank you:

To Randy, my biggest cheerleader...without your continued love, reassurance, and optimism this may have never been more than that little 2-page handout. Thank you for seeing my potential and bringing it out in me.

To Cyndi, my sister and Comma Queen, who continued to read and re-read and read again all of the many pages in this process. Thank you for your patience, encouragement, and corrections throughout this journey.

To Mom & Dad, Thank you for believing in me... without your love and support, this could not be possible.

To those who have come along side, linked arms with me, and shared in the every step creating **'She Believes'**. Your many prayers, the time and talents invested, and wisdom you have shared are priceless to me. Thank you for playing such a huge part in bringing this dream to life. Both this book and I am better for it.

INTRODUCTION

As we grow in stature and maturity, it is time to find a bicycle that fits you. We must take into consideration our physical size, abilities, and the purpose of the bicycle. A bicycle we would compete with in a race is drastically different than a bicycle we would use to troll around town.

Whether the bicycle is made for speed, to tackle trails, or for comfort, each one has unique physical characteristics and abilities to allow it to be used for its purpose. Sure...a trail bike could be used for speed and a racing bike could be used for a trip to the grocery, but it wouldn't be using it to its fullest potential.

Likewise, when embracing our God-given design, discovering our purpose is an important part of the process. God designed us with intention in his heart. From the beginning he had a plan in mind and designed us accordingly.

Some are built for speed, some are built for endurance, and still others for comfort. We are each uniquely Equipped for our custom purpose.

CONTENTS

Before the Wheels Start Spinning

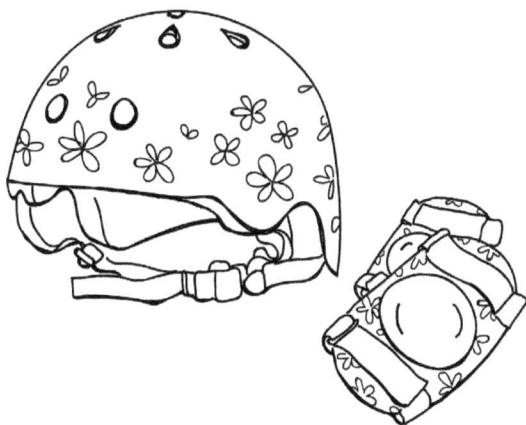

Before the Wheels Start Spinning

Have you ever tried to tell a child that she couldn't ride a bicycle when she believed full well that she could...even if she's never sat on a bicycle before? It doesn't matter to her if her feet can't quite reach the pedals or that the handlebars are too far away. It makes no difference if the bicycle is as big as she is. She has seen others ride, believes that she can, and is determined she will!

The process is different for each child. Some may take a long time as they grow into their ability, but others may take to it like a duck to water. Regardless of the time it takes, they will be riding like the best of them...if they just believe they can.

It starts with a dream...a longing in our heart... We dream to be loved, successful, totally committed, to feel beautiful, and to live a life with meaning and significance that makes a lasting impression. These dreams have been placed within our hearts by the Father Himself with the intention to draw us closer to Him and to reflect His Glory within us. These dreams can't be removed by repenting or suppressing them. We must seek the Father to fulfill them.

Whether you're just trying to figure out what life is all about or asking yourself if this is all there is, it's that longing that can start a journey to discovering who we are created to be and what our purpose is in life.

Then a decision...We have to make the decision that we are willing to walk with Father God on a journey of discovering who we are in His eyes. He is the one who has uniquely designed us with purpose in mind, and He is the one who can reveal not only the details of our design, but also the plans and dreams He has for us. We have to be prepared to believe His truths, even if you don't feel it or see it in the mirror...yet.

It's an amazing road you will travel on this journey. The sights, the lessons, the experiences...they not only can build your confidence and strengthen your relationship with the Father, but they can also bring freedom, healing, and a deeper understanding of His love.

I assure you that it is not too late. You have not missed your chance. You have not screwed up. Everything you have walked through up to this point...the good, bad, and ugly...has prepared you to walk into what the Father has prepared for you from the very beginning. It's His desire that you discover who you have been created to be and fulfill the dreams of your heart. They have not been hidden FROM you like a punishment but hidden FOR you to discover like a priceless treasure.

There is a purpose that has been custom created for you. It is a perfect fit. It is a place where you can shine and be fulfilled by just being yourself and doing what comes naturally. It is NOT by chance that you are reading this book right now. IT'S YOUR TIME to discover, embrace, and share your God-given design with the world.

Warning: This is not for the faint of heart. You may fall and scrape your knees. You may have to trek through some mud puddles and some hot dry days, but it is all worth it. Though some steps may be harder than others, trust that the Father knows exactly how high you can climb, when He can push you a little farther, when you need to play, and when you just need a little nap. He knows the best route for you to take, and He will get you there.

Don't get caught by the *Have* Trio..."Could Have", "Should Have", and "Would Have". Their mission is to keep you looking at the past. Instead you need to keep your eyes focused on the Father and the journey He has prepared for you. It is one of hope and abundance.

What will the journey look like? Because we are each different in the way we learn and grow, no two journeys will look the same, but the destination will be. First, the Father takes us on a treasure hunt to discover our God-given design. Then, He shows us how special that design is and why we should embrace what has been placed within us. Finally, we learn how it fits into our purpose...how we are to share that design with the world.

My Promise: This journey WILL change things in your life and the lives of others if you allow it. Just like that first time you rolled along on a bicycle. Life was never quite the same.

Remember, the Father is the one who knows you the best. He knows where you are heading and the best way to get you there. With this being the case, it is critical to get His input.

Now you might be thinking, "Wait a minute! I have to ask God for His input? What if I can't hear him? But what if I don't know how?"

One of the greatest benefits of being a child of the Father is hearing Him speak to us personally. We can't develop an intimate relationship with our heavenly Father without it. Can you imagine having a friendship or marriage where you can't talk with one another in one way or the other?

Although it is often easier for us to talk to the Father, the average Christian has a hard time hearing His voice. This is not the way He intended it to be. He speaks to every one of His children constantly, giving us all the information and guidance we need. It's not that the Lord has stopped speaking; it's just that we're not always hearing. We need to learn how to recognize His voice. It's priceless.

Here are a few tips to help:

- ❀Find a quiet place where you can take a few moments to breathe and still your own thoughts and emotions...my favorite place is the car.
- ❀Tune out the busyness and focus on the Father.
- ❀Ask Him to help you to recognize His voice and show you what is on His heart.
- ❀Read Scripture. Pray and think about what it is saying to you.
- ❀Journal or write out your prayers and the Father's answers.

In John 10, it says that His sheep...His child...hears His voice and follows him. The interesting thing about sheep is that they will only follow the shepherd whose voice they recognize. So what this is saying is that His child will not only hear His voice, but will recognize it enough to follow Him.

Think about the people you are around the most. When you hear them, you know who it is immediately. There may be some people you don't even have to hear speak; you recognize them by the sound of their walk, or the way they jingle the change in their pockets. This is the same way we are to be with the Father, to know Him so well that we hear Him and recognize Him.

In the same way He knows the best path to take us on in this journey, He knows the best way to speak to us. For some He could use scriptures and teachings, for others billboard signs and songs on the radio, and still others may hear Him through things they observe in nature. It may be like a still small voice or like a conversation with a friend. He speaks to each of us in the language that we hear the best.

Don't let fear get in the way of hearing. Watch out for fears that will tell you that you won't hear His voice, or if you do, you won't like what you hear. Push through them. The Father is not mad or sad, but loving and caring. He only wants the best for His children and withholds no good thing from us.

At the end of each chapter, I have included a decree of truth and a prayer.

She Believes… is a decree based on scripture that can strengthen us, prepare our hearts and minds for the purpose the Father has prepared for us. It is intended for you to speak it out loud as well as to hide it in your heart. It is not a positive affirmation or statement of wishful thinking; It is a statement of vision, purpose, and of God's truth.

Sometimes, it takes me speaking them over and over before they really start to sink in, and I accept them as truth. At first it feels odd, but as the scripture says... His word will not return void...it will be a light for the way we should go. I believe that as we speak the truth, it will transform and be a guide for us. (Is 55:11, Ps 119:105)

Prayer is so important in this process. There is no right or wrong way to talk with the Father. The prayers I have included are just a conversation starter or sample. For some, you may find the prayers a little different than just reciting the Lord's Prayer. They are specific to the journey. There is no magic formula in these prayers. The important thing is that they remind you to talk WITH the Father and take time to listen to what He is saying.

She Believes...

I believe that because I am a child of God, I hear and recognize the Father's voice. I believe that He will lead me in the best way for me because He knows me and is acquainted with all my ways. (John 10:27, Ps 139:1-6)

Prayer:

As I begin to seek you in this journey, reveal to me how you speak to me. Speak to me so often and so clearly that I learn to recognize your voice, and make any doubts that I hear you go away. Help me to trust that you do know me and have only the best in store for me.

Tricycles and Training Wheels
discovering your God-given design

Tricycles and Training Wheels
The How-To's

As you watch a child start to learn how to ride a bicycle you can see that they're torn between the desires to speed down the sideway like the older children do and uncertainty. The loving arms and reassuring words of parents helps to ease the tension.

They know that the child has everything she needs to ride, the right equipment, physical abilities, and even conditions. The child just needs to discover this as well. As she is getting up to speed, she will learn quickly what she is working with and is capable of. There's always a learning curve and times of trial and error but before long, she is pedaling down the sideway on her own.

It's the same for us as we begin this journey. We need to discover what we're working with. The Father has created each of us with a unique mix of natural gifts and talents, personality traits, strengths and weaknesses, likes and dislikes. These characteristics have all been weaved together with your life experiences to make you who you are.

- ❀**Natural gifts and talents**: those things that just come naturally, without a lot of effort at all. The difficult thing about natural abilities is that they are not always the easiest things for us to see in ourselves. We either assume that they are not special because everyone can do them, or they come so naturally, like breathing, that we don't even know we do them.

- ❀**Personality traits**: the way we behave, or our character. Being outgoing, reserved, friendly, confident, detailed, shy or driven can all be examples of these traits.

- ❀**Strengths**: things you just do really well. Keep in mind that these may not always be things that we love to do, but we are still good at doing them. A great example of this would be filing for me. I am great at setting up filing systems, but I HATE to file.

⊛**Weaknesses**: those things we think or have been told that we should be better at, but even with a lot of effort, we're just not.

⊛**Likes**: things you find joy in, that fascinate you. Things that cause us to lose track of time while doing and fill us with energy as we do them. It's those things that even if you have done them all day, you could just keep doing them.

⊛**Dislikes**: these are things that are like quicksand to us. They drain us mentally and physically. They are the things that you dread to do.

Each of these areas can give us a wealth of insight into how we have been intricately created by the Father. They are uncovered by asking both yourself and the Father questions.

Ask and Answer!

All it takes is a few thought-provoking questions to start the process of discovering your God-given design:

✸What are your strengths...what are you good at? Weaknesses?

✸What do you love to do? Hate?

✸If you could do anything without hindrances or limitations, what would it be?

Questions like these can open your eyes to many things, so ask yourself and *make* yourself answer them. Dig deep. Really push yourself to answer. Take time to let them steep. Ask others what they see in you. It can be helpful and eye opening as well. Friends and family see things that you may not see in yourself.

As I ponder over my questions, it helps me to journal my thoughts, feelings, and frustrations. Some days my journaling looks like a letter to a friend or a short story. Other days I fill pages with doodles, drawings, and bedazzled words. Regardless of what it looks like or how many pages I use, I always seem to uncover something by going through the process...sometimes answers...sometimes more questions. That's ok. Let the process take you to new discoveries about your hopes, dreams, and who you really were created to be.

I also ask the Father the same questions. I figure that since He has taken such great care to design and knit me together, I want to know what His design looks like from His perspective.

Just like parents with a new baby have dreams and plans for what the child will grow up to become, I believe that our Heavenly Father has big dreams and plans for us. I want to know what they are. You may be pleasantly surprised that the dreams the Father has for us are very similar to the dreams we have for ourselves...only bigger.

Be Honest

As you begin to answer these questions, some may be difficult and may bring up some unpleasant memories or emotions. Rather than making yourself dig deep for an honest answer, you may be tempted to answer with something other than what is true or avoid the question all together. DON'T let yourself do it!! Hold yourself accountable or find someone who will help you be accountable. You owe it to yourself to be completely honest.

This was really hard for me at first. When a question got tough or hit a sore spot in my heart, I would let myself "off the hook" or jump to another question that seemed easier or less painful. Of course, if I was asking someone else the same questions, I would expect an honest response rather than a vague answer that danced around the subject like I was giving myself.

If you find that this is the case, ask the question: Why? Why am I avoiding it? Why does it bring up emotions? Ask The Father to reveal things that you may not be seeing. Ask Him to help you answer truthfully.

It took some time for me to realize the reason I was doing this. I didn't value my dreams and desires. I also found that I answered the way I thought I should...the "correct" way, as if it was going to be judged by someone else...Boy, was that an eye opener!

Bottom line: There are no wrong answers. Be honest with yourself in answering questions. This is NOT a test. The only person you will cheat with dishonesty or avoidance is yourself. The more thought and time you take to answer the questions honestly, the better the results you will get.

Clarify

When I began this process, I started with listing things I love. Traveling was on the top of my list. Then someone asked me what it was about traveling that I loved. At first I thought...What? I have to dig deeper? I was stumped for a while. Traveling was always my "go-to" answer, but I had never really thought about WHY I loved traveling.

I bet that if I looked over your answers, I could ask you the same question. What is it about ____ that you love? When I started digging, I discovered that there were two things that stuck out that I loved: the planning and packing process, and talking to new people. I later could see how this goes right along with how I was designed.

Look at your answers. Can you get more specific and detailed? If so, do it. This can be both difficult and eye opening, but worth it for the information it can reveal.

Other tools

Assessment tools like *Disc, Strengths Finder, Myers-Briggs and How to Fascinate* can also help you articulate and understand your design. With descriptive words like direct, outgoing, consistent, analytical, driven, patient, and influential, they give you a clearer description.

In addition to helping you discover your design, the assessments can help you better understand others. We all process information differently, have different communication styles, and priorities. Where some are driven by respect and are task oriented, others are driven by admiration and building relationships.

When I began to understand this, it was like a light bulb came on for the first time. Not only did I see my design more clearly, but I started to understand others more clearly as well. I could see how at times I had gotten hurt by others just because I did not understand that they saw things from a different perspective. Neither was wrong or right, just different. When I finally saw where they were coming from and the motivation behind what they said to me, it was much easier to forgive them of the pain they had caused.

Can you see how considering the differences of others can bring freedom and healing? It could be really easy for a person to get offended and hurt if there is a misperception of personalities. By learning more about ourselves and others, it can bring a freedom, understanding, and appreciation of differences when working and relating to people.

She Believes...

I believe I am loved by the Father and that if I seek answers, He hears my prayers.
(Proverbs 15:28-29, Matthew 7:7-8, Romans 8:35-39, 1 John 5:14)

Prayer:

Father, as I start asking questions, help me to have the patience to work through them. If questions hit tender spots in my heart where I have experienced pain, please comfort me, encourage me, and help me to push past it to uncover the treasures you have placed within me. Guard my heart and mind from the fear and insecurity that may come with my answers. Fill this time with a joy for discovering the treasures about myself and drawing closer to you.

Streamers & Spinners

embracing your God-given design

Streamers & Spinners
Discovering and Embracing Your God-given design

I remember my first "big girl" bicycle. It was a shiny red number with a cool banana seat. It was important to me that everyone knew it was mine. I didn't want it to look like other bikes. I added streamers, a bell, and spinners on the wheel spokes. Not only could you see that it was my bike, but because of its distinctive sound, you could *hear* that it was my bike.

Our God-given design is the same way. When we begin to discover who we are, we find that there's a freedom and a joy that comes in being authentic. We no longer want to be like everyone else on the block, but instead we embrace our differences.

Let's look at some areas that will help you discover facets of your unique design.

Your Name

Just like the names of products, we associate a name with an attribute. When we hear Prada, we think of high fashion. When we hear Apple, we think innovative. The same can go for given names. It's interesting to learn what people's names mean. So many times I see how they really reflect who the person is or the life they lead. In biblical times, great thought went into the naming a child. It was a reflection of who you were in a family or spoke of the future the child would have.

Some of my favorites names that I studied are Ronna: mighty counselor or ruler, Sarah: princess, Nicole: person of victory, and of course Melissa: honey bee. *Buzz Buzz*...Google the meaning of your name, see what you find. Also pray about your name. Ask the Father how your name relates to who you are. It may just shed light on your God-given design in a fun way.

Your Family

Not only was it important to the Father to give you specific gifts, talents, and skills, it was equally as important to Him that you were born into the right environment. He selected both your environment and the season you would be born.

The saying "the apple doesn't fall far from the tree" is true in many respects. It doesn't have to be referring to negative traits, but instead, it can help uncover many good things. It wasn't until I started to figure out who I was created to be; that I realized I had many traits and talents that I saw in my mother, my grandmother, and past generations.

A gift of music, a love of craftsmanship, and a knack for organizing and design are all traits I can trace back through generations. These are a part of my family blessing that I can choose to embrace.

Are there common threads that you can see throughout your family history? Does it seem that your family is known for something unique? It is so much fun to uncover little things that otherwise would seem common, knowing that it brings clarity of another facet to your design.

Yes, there are some traits that are not so positive. Just because it's part of our family history doesn't mean we have to take it on ourselves. This is when knowing the truth about what God says helps us to filter the truth from the lies and the blessings from the curses.

Ask the Father what He sees. Are there family blessings that may have been dropped through the generations that he intended for you to walk in.

Your Experiences

We have to walk through an array of experiences, some good and some not so good. It's these experiences that have shaped us into who we are today...just like how a tree is shaped by its environment.

Our experiences have caused us to grow in strength of character and faith, and it's by these experiences that we can help others. What have you had to overcome? What have you had to learn through your experiences? Whether you've been trudging through the mud or splashing around in the puddles, you now have the opportunity, with your new knowledge, understanding, and compassion, to be there for others experiencing similar things.

Your Reflection

In the same way that the Father intricately planned your design, he also planned the reflection you see in the mirror. We may not understand the purpose or plan behind how we look, but it was still important to the Father to give us our distinctive physical attributes. Blue eyes, red hair, and rounded nose, short, tall, thin or stout: He selected them specifically for you. It is all a part of His overall design.

And as part of His design, we need to embrace it as well. No, we may not look like the supermodel in a magazine or an Olympic gold medalist, but we are who He created us to be.

Your Wiring

Inside every acorn is everything it needs to grow into a mighty oak tree. The little acorn doesn't have to hope to become an oak. It doesn't even have to perform or be good enough to become a tree. All it needs is the proper resources and a suitable environment.

There are millions of oak trees. Within those, there are about 60 different species, and yet none are exactly alike. Each have characteristics that tell us they are oaks, such as the bark, shape of leaves, and wood grain. Because each tree has also been shaped by outside influences, no two trees are identical. The amount of water, light, and environment all influence the tree's development.

Like the acorn, everything you need...skill, personality, passions, and dreams...has been placed within you from the beginning to achieve what you were created to be. You are wired with a wonderful collection of gifts, talents, personality traits, and experiences that has equipped you to become the best "YOU".

Your Voice

In addition to wiring, God has placed within you a voice...a unique expression. When it's released into the world in a positive way, it can speak hope, instruction, comfort, encouragement, truths, and so on. It doesn't necessarily come from our mouths, but always comes from our heart. Our voice can change atmospheres around us.

❀Observe the voices around you. How does it affect you and others around them?

❀Do you notice a change in the atmosphere when different people speak?

❀When reading a Facebook post, are you encouraged, agitated?

✹When you watch a commercial are you motivated to take action?

Discovering my voice was very difficult for me. Because of fears and pains from past experiences, I truly believed that I was unable to communicate well, my voice was not worth being heard, and that no one would listen if I did speak up. One day the Father took me to this verse:

> *"O my dove, in the clefts of the rock, in the crannies of the cliff, let me see your face, let me hear your voice, for your voice is sweet,and your face is lovely. "*
> Song of Solemn 2:14 (ESV)

There is something magical that happens when a father tells a daughter that he wants to hear what she has to say...even the littlest of details. At that point, I knew that it didn't make a difference if I had a fantastic singing voice, some deep revelation to share, or just wanted to say "Hi". My Father God not only liked to hear me but, *wanted* to hear me. My voice is sweet!

The fears of not having a beautiful sounding voice, not being eloquent, and what others may think melted away. I knew that I had the ear of someone who loved me dearly.

Have you discovered your voice? Are you willing to freely share with others?

Your Thoughts

Our minds should be like a high-end condominium protected by a doorman or a gated community protected by a security guard. People don't just freely come in without ownership or permission. They're questioned and scrutinized. "What's your name? Why are you here? What's your purpose?" In the same way, we must interrogate thoughts that try to get into our minds. If they don't measure up with the truth...they're outta there!

Over the years, I let negative thoughts not just come in but move in. They would play in my head like a tape recording, reminding me again and again that I was not smart enough, not good enough, undeserving, that I looked foolish, others would not like me, and I was a failure. Get the picture?

Not only would I listen to them, but I would believe and agree with the lies. I would not step out of my comfort zone and try new things because I was afraid that these thoughts were right. Of course, if they were right, then why even bother trying.

An eviction notice must be served! We must combat the negative with the positive, what God says is true. What does God say about you? Find scriptures that speak the truth opposite the lies and declare them over you.

This is the perfect time to start a list of scriptures that tell you who you are in Christ. This list can become a great tool to memorize and to refer back to when you need reminders.

Your Words

It's not what you answer to, it's what you call yourself that matters most.
Ilesha "Coco" Graham

What do you say about yourself? How do you define yourself? There is power in speaking and hearing truth. Become aware of what you say to yourself and to others. It is time we speak up and tell ourselves the truth about ourselves and the situations we are in.

Create signs or cards with encouraging words and phrases about who you are, how great you are doing, and where you are going. Put them in places you see them every day and read them OUT LOUD! Your ears need to hear it. Read them until you have them memorized and then change them out with new phrases.

It is time to tell ourselves what is really true about us...even if we don't feel it or see it in the mirror yet. By both reading and speaking aloud the scriptures and declarations, you are evicting the lies and reprogramming the recordings with the truth. It also equips you with a powerful arsenal that helps you stand firm against doubt and fear....successfully!

What You Believe

If you think you can, you can. And if you think you can't, You're right.
Mary Kay Ash

Regardless of whether it is positive or negative, the things we believe and see ourselves doing...or not doing...is exactly what we become and achieve. Think about the things you believe about yourself and your abilities.

❀Are they a reflection of what others have told you?

❀Are they positive and uplifting or negative and self-sabotaging?

Because of an incident at birth, I have never had full dexterity or strength in my right hand. From the beginning, I was limited physically from doing certain things...unless I really set my mind to it, of course. Side note: Did you know we live in a world where nearly everything is right handed?...like a jack-in-the-box...Ugh!

I've had to find some pretty unique and create ways to achieve things if I wanted to do them, like playing piano and driving.

I remember the first time I rode a 10-speed. Not thinking about how the brakes worked, I went speeding down the road. It wasn't until I had to stop that I found out how important hand brakes were. As I lay on the ground I could have given up and never rode again, but that was not an option. I liked riding a bicycle too much.

It took a some thought and a little ingenuity, but I believed there was a way. Once I figured out that all it would take was changing which hand controlled the front brakes, I was on my way. And never flew face first over the handlebars again.

What is it you believe about yourself and your abilities? Remember that it is best to go by what the Father says about you and your abilities, rather than what past experiences tell you.

Inspiration

Along my journey, I have come across people who are walking in their purpose and passion. As I observe them, be around them, and learn from them, they give me a priceless commodity... PERMISSION TO BE ME! They may be nothing like me, but they model what it looks like to celebrate their design and walk in purpose.

Looking at the people you admire most and are drawn to can shed light on many facets of you.

- ❀Who are they? Why do you admire or feel drawn to them?
- ❀Are these attributes you would like to see in yourself?
- ❀Do they have similar gifts and abilities?

I believe there is a benefit in observing and learning from others that are a few steps ahead of us. We can learn from their mistakes and successes. By looking at several different examples, you can see how others embrace their design from different angles and viewpoints. Just because someone has similar skills and talents, doesn't mean your walk will look exactly like theirs, but knowing that there are many ways to use what you are given can only add to your journey.

She Believes . . .

I believe I am beautiful. The Father has put a great deal of thought into every detail of my design for a unique purpose and plan.
Psalms 139:13, Song of Solomon 1:15, Jeremiah 29:11-13

Prayer:

Father, reveal the different facets of my design and the way you see them. Teach me why you made me in this way. Help me to see those things I don't really like about myself through your eyes and embrace who you created me to be.

Are there things that I have believed are not true? Teach me your truth. What do you say about me and my situations? Direct me to scriptures that I can memorize that will evict what is not true and will build and strengthen me on my journey.

Bring others into my life that will inspire and encourage me. Take away my disbelief and my doubts. Help me to have the faith I need to believe.

Flat Tires and Pot Holes

what to watch out for

Flat Tires and Pot Holes
What to watch out for

Now that we are getting a little more comfortable with the ride that we have been on of discovering our God-given design, we need to discuss some of the pesky things that can happen along the way.

As I learned to ride a bicycle, one of the things that my dad was adamant about was that I learned how to use a tire pump for a flat tire. He wanted me to be prepared just like I want you to be for what may be ahead. If you know the signs of what to look out for you will know how to handle the flats and obstacles when they come up and possibly avoid them altogether.

Limitations: Real or Imagined?

Did you know that the limitations and hindrances in front of you may no longer be valid and are just in your mind? I will give you a great example. Have you ever wondered how they keep an elephant from running away? Basically the trainer ties a baby elephant to a large stake with a heavy chain and shackle. The baby elephant tries and tries to pull away but the shackle causes pain. After a while, the elephant gives up trying. She grows up believing that she is limited in where she can go and what she can do, even when that is no longer true. As an adult elephant, she is VERY capable of pulling out the stake or breaking the chain, but she won't even try.

Sad, huh? You may be facing some limitations just like the elephant. Some have been created because you have tried something in the past, and you got hurt. You may have been given limitations as a child for your own safety, but they no longer apply today. I see it like this. Many limitations come down to what we believe. As we take them on as truth, it's like adding links to a paper chain.

Can you picture Arnold Schwarzenegger being held down with paper chains? It's ridiculous, but these chains can hold us back from seeing ourselves correctly and moving forward into purpose. Yes, paper chains are easily torn, but because we choose to believe the lies, we trick our minds into thinking they are made of heavy iron. We are the ones that give the chains the power to hold us back.

So what do you do about paper chains? Go back to the beginning of the ABC's. Ask questions to help you identify limitations and the lies you have believed were true. Seek out what is true. What does God say about you? What does God say about the situation? Repent for believing the lies. Begin telling yourself the truth...those things God says....even if you don't see it in the mirror quite yet.

You may have to go through this process many times. As things come up and as we grow, we have to ask new questions that uncover steps we didn't know we had to take in the beginning. After this process, you may still feel that the lie is true, but let's face it; sometimes you just have to put on your big girl panties and believe what the Father says.

Stay Focused

As in any journey, there are obstacles to overcome, unforeseen twists to unravel and unfamiliar turns to navigate. In these times, we must keep our eyes on the larger picture...what we are working towards.

Veering off course only 2 degrees can cause a ship to end up miles from its desired destination. It's important to keep in sight what you're out to do... discover, embrace, and share your God-given design.

Be sure to stop and evaluate where you are from time-to-time. Are you still following the Father? Are you working on things He wants you to spend time on, or have you gotten slightly off track.

One way to tell you are veering off track is that everything feels forced, or like you have just stepped into quicksand. Joy and peace are zapped from you! If you find that this has happened, take a moment, breathe, and remember that the Father is leading you through this journey. Ask Him to show you what caused you to stray and to help you get refocused.

Comparison

There is another hazard that comes with wandering eyes. That is when we start looking at other people's journey. As we look at what they're doing and how far they have come, we start comparing ourselves to them. DON'T! We all have to start at the beginning. The people you admire, the people with similar passions all started in the same place...the beginning. We all have to learn to walk before we can run...or ride.

Comparison is a swindler and a liar. His mission is to convince you to trade the thrill of this journey for hopelessness and doubt. He tells you lies that make you feel inferior and question if you will ever find your purpose. That liar knows the authority you will walk in when you discover who you are created to be. He wants nothing more than to make you want to throw your hands up and quit before you even start.

My suggestion: Don't give Comparison the time of day! Your journey, though it may be similar to others, will be as unique as you. Don't let anyone or anything convince you otherwise.

How Others View Your Journey

Just as each one of us is unique, we also can see things differently. Do not assume people always understand the journey we're on. It may not always look like what others think they should. That is not a bad thing. We just have to understand this as we share it with others.

Here is an example. Because I am someone who like to process through things verbally, as I started my journey, I wanted to talk to everyone around me about it. I would ask them questions about what they saw as strengths and weaknesses in me. I would share my dream of wanting to do something that used my talents and skills in a greater way and that made an impact on others. I would tell them how I had found others that were doing this and how they inspired me to pursue that.

It didn't take me long to realize that what I was saying and what they were understanding were two different things. I was looking to embrace my God-given design and live with purpose. They thought that I was just miserable at my job and wanted something different because I was bored. For me the success of this journey wasn't based on finding a new job or a new exciting

39

project. For me, it was about finding my passion and purpose.

To avoid being misunderstood, be clear on what you're trying to accomplish and who you share it with. The measurement of success is defined only by you.

Look for those individuals who recognize, speak into, and encourage you to reach your potential. These are the people that will catapult you ahead.

Falling Down

Getting tripped up, falling down, and failing is a part of the process of moving forward. No, you may not always get it right the first time, or even the second, but what's important is your attitude and that you are making an effort.

Look at Thomas Edison...it took him 10,000 tries to create the light bulb. When asked about his failures, he replied, "I have not failed. I've just found 10,000 ways that won't work. "

Yes, you may trip and fall and even fail, but it doesn't have to be the end of the ride. Get back up, dust yourself off, and take a go at it again. Don't let a fear of failing rob you of this journey and the joys it will bring. Instead let it propel you towards your purpose. Press through. Do the things that cause you to be afraid. When you do, fear will lose its power to hold you back. As you overcome fear, you will be able to help others tackle fear as well.

Don't Ride Alone

We get so close and engaged with what we are doing at times that we can overlook key pieces. Being a task-oriented person, one thing I overlook is that the Father never intended for me to walk this journey without Him; it's a partnership. I get it in my mind what needs to be done, and off I go, leaving Him in the dust.

He desires to work alongside us every day rather than just tell us what to do then meet us at the end. What are things you easily overlook? It's good to stop and make sure you don't walk off without the Father at your side.

Running on "E"

From time to time, we can get so driven that we forget to stop and get refueled. We all need to take time to rest, get refreshed, and become inspired again. This is a great time to "let your hair down" and play. Do activities that you enjoy. Visit places that inspire you.

Relax. This is not a sprint but a lifelong journey. You'll not find out everything about the reasons you are created one way or the other all at once. It is a process of growth and maturity that will develop over seasons.

Give yourself permission to be present in the now and not always thinking six steps ahead. It will come together in God's perfect time. Just believe that He is in control and that He is faithful to complete the good work He started.

Remember that the Father is not a task master that simply gives orders to watch and see if we obey or fail. Instead He is a loving Father that wants to see us excel in life and grow in relationship with Him.

Slow down and enjoy the ride.

I Just Don't WANT To!

"Procrastination is the assassin of passion!"
Wendy K Walters

In life there are always those things we just don't like or don't want to do. We hem and haw around not getting anywhere. But why?

A few reasons for this might be that the things we are facing are:

- ❀ Overwhelming: It can be new; we don't know where to begin or how to proceed; we don't know how to emotionally deal with it; and it just seems intimidating.
- ❀ Unimportant: It seems insignificant or unnecessary. Don't underestimate where steps that seem unimportant or too small to matter can take you.
- ❀ Unpleasant: We just don't like doing them.

In any journey there are things that we feel apprehensive about, we are not sure how to do, we are afraid of, or we just plain don't want to do. We would rather throw in the towel and quit than press onward. But don't! Ask yourself these questions...

- ❀ If I don't pursue this dream, will I regret it in 10 years?
- ❀ If not now, WHEN?
- ❀ What is stopping me from moving forward?

Don't Give Up! Keep Pedaling!

If you are like me, you would like to be at the end of the journey doing, being, or enjoying the fruits of this labor, BUT, as they say, getting there is half the fun. The journey as a whole can be daunting, so if you find yourself getting overwhelmed, remember to take it one step at a time. Each step, no matter how big or small, will take you to the next step. Let's face it, there are some days when our impatience gets the better of us, and all we want to see are results. In those times, remember that this is about the journey of discovering and spending quality time with Father. It just takes persistence, consistency, and a little patience.

> Persevere: to persist in anything undertaken; maintain a purpose in spite of difficulty, obstacles, or discouragement; continue steadfastly

> Consistent: always behaving in the same way; of the same quality; especially good each time; continuing to happen or develop in the same way

Persistence will get you there. When you are not sure you can continue on, press on! It doesn't matter how slow you go, as long as you keep moving. Your persistence will pay off. It's the deliberate, intentional, and purposeful actions that will propel you into your purpose.

Consistence will keep you there. The more you do something, the easier it becomes. It becomes like second nature. It no longer takes the same effort that it did in the beginning. It is not that the action has changed, but you have. Consistency may not always be fun, but it is highly effective in achieving your goals and dreams.

I wonder how many times I have given up and quit when I was so close to what I had been working for. Don't give up! You may only be two inches from finding the treasures the Father has hidden for you to find.

She Believes . . .

I believe that because I listen to the Father and His direction, I will walk securely and my foot will not stumble. Because He is faithful, I am hidden and sheltered in Him.
Psalms 91, Proverbs 1:33, Proverbs 3:23

Prayer

Father, open my eyes to see the limitations that are no longer valid in my life. Where have I believed lies as truth and willingly put on paper chains? Help me to destroy my paper chains and walk in Your Truth.

Help me not to get ahead or lose focus of you. Remind me that it's not a sprint but a journey that you want to share with me. Forgive me for when I have just been focused on the task and forgotten to include You in my day. Help me to recognize and acknowledge You each step of the way.

Give me the stamina and tenacity to continue when things get tough. Wrap Your arms around me when I am weary and weak.

Cruisers

celebrating your God-given design

Cruisers
Celebrating Your God-given Design

As we grow in stature and maturity, it is time to find a bicycle that fits you. We must take into consideration our physical size, abilities, and the purpose of the bicycle. A bicycle we would compete with in a race is drastically different than a bicycle we would use to troll around town.

Whether the bicycle is made for speed, to tackle trails, or for comfort, each one has unique physical characteristics and abilities to allow it to be used for its purpose. Sure...a trail bike could be used for speed and a racing bike could be used for a trip to the grocery, but it wouldn't be using it to its fullest potential.

Likewise, when embracing our God-given design, discovering our purpose is an important part of the process. God designed us with intention in His heart. From the beginning He had a plan in mind and designed us accordingly.

Some are built for speed, some are built for endurance, and still others for comfort. We are each uniquely equipped for our custom purpose.

Round or Square?

"You don't alter a Vera Wang [dress] to fit you; you alter yourself to fit Vera!" (Bride Wars)

The first time · I heard this, I giggled and thought to myself "So true", but then the meaning sunk in. What?! How absurd to think women believe they have to change their bodies in order to fit a dress! Then it hit me... too many of us are guilty of doing the same thing, maybe not with a Vera Wang, but worse...our lives.

Rather than discovering, developing, and walking in the design the Father has tailored specifically for us, we try with all of our strength to change who we are in hopes to satisfy the longings of our heart, or simply to fill the needs...like a round peg in a square hole.

Yes, it is possible to get a round peg into a square hole, but one of two things has to happen. Either we have to cut off so much from the sides of the peg that it's no longer round, or the peg only fills out the center of the square but leaves the corners empty.

We relinquish our dreams, desires, and even our design to fill the voids and meet expectations. It works for a little while, but it's exhausting and takes a toll on us mentally, physically, and spiritually.

Eventually, we either return to being that round peg we were designed to be, or we lose sight of ourselves altogether. If we don't understand and embrace our "roundness", it can lead to feelings of hopelessness and failing.

A Perfect Fit?

I have always been the social honeybee of my family. My Papaw taught me that there were no strangers, just friends I had not met yet. I have always enjoyed meeting new people and bringing people together.

Like a honeybee, I flit from one person to another spending only a few minutes with each one. As we talk, instinctively I store bits of information that I gather, what they do, what they like, etc. in my mental rolodex. I just know that it could be useful sometime. When I hear someone mention a need or an interest in something...just like breathing, my mind goes to work thinking about other people or places I can connect them with. Again like the honeybee, I go from one to another, cross-pollinating, so everyone can be fruitful. It is who I am and even what my name means... go figure!

The funny thing is that I didn't know this about myself. I thought it was terrible that in a room full of people, I couldn't stay focused enough to have a long and in-depth conversation with even a few people. I was always distracted by the pull to talk with everyone. I didn't fit the image, or the square hole, I thought I should. I apologized all the time, especially to my friends that preferred to sit and talk with only a few.

It wasn't until a friend pointed it out to me that I discovered this was how I was wired, and that we should never apologize for the way God designs us. She proceeded to tell me that anytime she needed to know who to talk to or where to go for something, I was always the person with the information.

WHAT? This was ok? I was floored! This started opening my eyes to see that we are each wired in a unique way. We each have a unique purpose in the body...a part that no one else will ever be able to use like we can. Our unique design and experiences, both the good and the bad, have been, and will continue to prepare us for what the Father has planned and dreamed for us from the very beginning.

Just the Way We Are

Are there certain things that you feel like you need to change, but it seems to be "just the way you are"? Think about it. Look back at your answers. Are there common traits that stick out at you? Think about past experiences. Are there things you have apologized for over and over? Could these be traits that God has put within you to fit in a specific place in the body of Christ?

As we are told in the Bible, the body of Christ is made up of many members. We each have a specific role within that body. Not everyone is intended to be the hands, the feet, or even the ears. Can you imagine how effective THAT would be?

It's tempting at times to look at other roles and want to play their part because they seem more glamorous or exciting, especially when we're not certain where we fit in. But if we are trying to fill someone else's role, it leaves the role that is intended for us unoccupied.

By trying to change or suppress our God-given design to be someone we're not is like saying to God that His design isn't right or good enough. These are lies that tell us we need to change. We need to recognize that we have been believing lies as if they were true and ask God for forgiveness. After receiving His forgiveness, ask Him to teach us the truth about who we are and to show us where we do fit perfectly.

Embracing who you are can be both exciting and freeing at the same time. It's amazing how things look when we start to see them from the Father's point of view. What was once an area where I felt inapt, inferior, and a failure, is now the area I celebrate and consider one of my greatest strengths.

It's Not Just About Me?

Our purpose is rooted in our passion...that thing we find that ignites us. It is not intended to be kept to ourselves, hoarded away, but to be shared with others for their benefit, not ours.

In the same way a full moon reflects the glory of the sun, we are designed to reflect God's glory. It is by the posture of our heart and alignment we have with the Father that we do this. It is not always about preaching from a pulpit or being a missionary to the nations...though some are made for that. We are to reflect His glory through our God-given design.

As we begin to walk authentically in who we are created to be, it gives those around us permission to be who they are created to be as well. And with the voice, that unique expression, that we've been given can bring glory to God.

Meet the Designer

This journey is not only about learning how you are designed to be, but it's also about getting intimately acquainted with the Designer Himself. Through both the mountaintop experiences where He shows you the precious things He has planned in your future and the valley experiences where He carries you to healing from the pains from the past, you will share experiences that allow you to know Him in a deeper way.

By sharing these experiences, the Father will show you His heart and prove that He is who He says He is. Just like how any friendship or marriage is made stronger by sharing both the joys and sorrows, your relationship with the Father will be strengthened. Because we are made in His image, it only makes sense that as we learn more about who we are, we learn more about who He is.

You've Come a Long Way

"Memorial stones are the pathway to the past that directs us to the future."
Dallas Eggemeyer

Testimonies are a powerful thing. They not only remind us of where we've been and how far we've come, but how good and faithful the Father is. When shared with others, they not only build our faith, but they have the power to encourage and build the faith of others.

One of my favorite examples of mile markers is Joshua's pile of rocks found in the fourth chapter of Joshua. He had the stones that the priests stood on as Israel crossed the Jordan River into the Promised Land collected and brought to their camp. The stones served as a reminder of how God brought them across the river.

I could picture the grandfather taking the hand of a small child and leading her to this pile of stones and saying as he touched a rock, "This is the very stone I stood on when God brought us across the Jordan.

Sometimes our testimonies seem insignificant in comparison to someone else's, but never underestimate their power. Regardless of whether or not they seem significant to you, they may have the power to speak life and hope to someone else. They have the potential to cause someone else to think "if they can do it, so can I".

She Believes...

I believe that God designed and formed me completely; He placed within me skills, talents, and characteristics specifically with a purpose and plan in mind that will reflect His glory to others.
(Psalms 139:13-16, Isaiah 60:1-3, Jeremiah 29:11)

Prayer:

Father, are there places that I have tried to alter myself to fit a perception of what I thought was acceptable? Have I tried to change to gain the favor of others by being something I wasn't? Are there lies I have believed about who I am and how I was designed?

Reveal Your plans, purpose, and dreams for my life. Help me to celebrate where I've been and look forward to where I'm going.

Bicycles Built for Two

it's about a relationship

Bicycles Built for Two
It's About a Relationship

Let's Do It Together!

Riding a bicycle by yourself can be a rewarding experience, but riding tandem adds a whole new dimension. It allows two riders that have different strengths and abilities to share an experience. A stronger rider doesn't have to wait for the slower one, nor does the slower rider have to struggle to try to keep up with the faster rider. It is a joint venture...a partnership.

There is a romantic and picturesque image in our heads of what riding tandem could be like, but there's a lot of teamwork and communication involved. It's not a situation of driver and passenger, but both riders that are equal participants with individual responsibilities.

The rider in the front is called the pilot. He is responsible for controlling the bike and also setting the pace that they will travel. It is important that he earn the confidence of the second rider. Because the second rider cannot see the road directly in front of them, the pilot has the responsibility of warning the second rider of bumps in the road and sudden changes, so she can be prepared and brace herself.

The one in the back seat is called the stoker. Her responsibilities are to help generate power, keep in line with the bicycle, and lean with the pilot. It is crucial that she NOT attempt to steer. This can cause serious accidents.

An experienced tandem team develops a special level of nonverbal communication. After hundreds of miles together, tandem riders find themselves coasting at the same time, shifting without the need of discussion, and maneuvering smoothly even at slow speeds. There is a fluidity, balance, and rhythm to their team work. Both riders must be synchronized...both when pedaling and when coasting.

One of the biggest hurdles of riding tandem is when the stoker losses confidence and becomes scared. Can you see the parallels in riding tandem to the journey the Father wants to share with us?

Too often I have found myself wanting to share the ride but not wanting to give up control. There's a security I find in knowing what to expect and where I'm going. I want to be the pilot. I LIKE to be the pilot!

To give up control is probably one of the hardest things for me to do. I struggled with believing He would not hold back any good thing from me and that He always had the best intentions for me. Giving up control meant I have to trust that the Father is not only faithful, but capable of getting me where I need to go. I have to believe that He is who He says He is and that His ways are better than mine.

It is impossible to grab ahold of the dreams the Father has for us if we have our hands clenched around the dreams we have for ourselves. The dreams to be loved, successful, totally committed, to feel beautiful, and to live a life with meaning and significance that makes a lasting impression are all dreams that the Father has placed within our hearts. It isn't until we give them back to Him that they can be fully realized.

This journey isn't intended for us to simply discover our God-given design so we would know what kind of job we should look for. Instead it's about learning how the Father sees us and how He uniquely designed us to fit into the body of Christ.

As we pedal along with him, our faith grows, and our ability to believe the truth increases. We can put our full confidence in Him...ringing our bells and honking our horns...knowing full well that when we walk in our God-given design we reflect His Glory.

So...this is an invitation. Are you ready to take the ride of your life?

It starts with one question...

what do you believe?

Arise, my love, my beautiful one, *and*

ride with me.

Song of Solomon 2:13 (Italicized mine)

Hello my friend!

Thank you so much for sharing this journey of discovering your God-given design with me. Wouldn't it be great if we could sit down and chat about it over a great cup of coffee? Until then, I hope we can stay connected in other ways.

Come over for a visit at www.missyhelderman.com. When you subscribe by e-mail, you'll get free encouraging messages from me sent right into your inbox. You can also connect with me on Facebook and Twitter as @MissyHelderman

Before I go, can I ask a favor? I'd love a review of She Believes... Uniquely Designed with Purpose in Mind. Good, Bad OR Ugly... I would appreciate your feedback on www.missyhelderman.com.

As a new author, reviews are extremely important to the success of this book. As a reader, you have the power to make it or break it. Would you please take a moment to voice your opinion? In doing this, you may help someone else find She Believes... and start the ride of her life.

Thanks again for reading She Believes... and spending time with me.

xoxo
Missy

www.ingramcontent.com/pod-product-compliance
Lightning Source LLC
Chambersburg PA
CBHW071625040426
42452CB00009B/1496